Scroll Saw
Mosaics

by Frank Droege

Fox
Chapel Publishing Co. Inc.

1970 Broad Street • East Petersburg, PA 17520 • www.carvingworld.com

Publisher: Alan Giagnocavo
Editor: Ayleen Stellhorn
Desktop Specialist: Linda L. Eberly, Eberly Designs Inc.
Cover Design: Linda Forrest

ISBN 1-56523-160-0
Library of Congress Card Number 2001092787

To order your copy of this book,
please remit the cover price
plus $3.00 shipping to:
Fox Chapel Publishing Company
Book Orders
1970 Broad Street
East Petersburg, PA 17520

Or visit us on the web at
www.scrollsawer.com

Manufactured in the United States
10 9 8 7 6 5 4 3 2 1

Because working with a scroll saw inherently includes the risk of injury and damage, this book cannot guarantee that creating the projects described herein is safe for everyone. For this reason, this book is sold without warranties or guarantees of any kind, express or implied, and the publisher and author disclaim any liability for any injuries, losses or damages caused in any way by the content of this book or the reader's use of the tools needed to complete the projects presented herein. The publisher and the author urge all scrollsawers to thoroughly review each project and to understand the use of any tools involved before beginning any project.

Table of Contents

About the Author

Designing scroll saw mosaic patterns and pieces can be described as a passionate pastime for **Frank Droege.** Frank's first love is painting. Over the years, he has won numerous awards as a traditional painter. Frank studied under George Vail from the Haddonfield Art League and under Max Gottlieb at the Fleisher Art Memorial in Philadelphia, Pennsylvania. He currently paints miniature art and has recently become an award-winning artist in the field. Frank lives in Voorhees, New Jersey, with his wife and daughters. Inquiries about his artwork can be addressed directly to Frank at 306 Kresson-Gibbsboro Road, Voorhees, NJ 08043.

Basic Cutting Techniques

Scroll saw mosaics are a variation on scroll saw segmentation techniques. Simply saw the pattern pieces, round the edges and glue the pieces back together on a ⅛ in. backing. The rounded corners give the finished artwork the illusion of ceramic tile mosaics.

Because the finished pieces are painted, I recommend using softwoods, such as white pine or white cedar. A no. 2 scroll saw blade, reverse tooth, is ideal for cutting mosaics. The reverse tooth eliminates tear out and reduces the number of burs that will need to be sanded off the bottom of the piece.

To round the corners of the cut pieces, I use a hand-held grinder or micro motor tool, fitted with a ¼ in. sanding band. Round the corners to a uniform ⅟₃₂ in. to ⅟₁₆ in. radius.

When the pieces are rounded to your satisfaction, paint each piece according to the suggested color scheme or with colors of your choosing. I use brightly colored acrylic paints to complete the look of a tile mosaic. All of the pattern pieces in this book are numbered to correspond to a suggested color scheme. Use the color pictures of the finished mosaics on the inside covers as reference.

Glue the pieces to the backing with yellow wood glue. Create any additional fine details, such as eyes and antennae, with paint or a woodburner; then finish the entire piece with acrylic varnish. Hang the piece for display with saw-tooth hooks or wire and eye hooks.

Remember, you can simplify any piece by removing lines and decreasing the number of pieces in any pattern.

- **Step One:** Cut two pieces of wood a little larger than the pattern you wish to scroll: a ⅛-in.-thick piece for the backer and a ⅜-in.-thick piece for the pattern.
- **Step Two:** Glue the pattern to the ⅜ in. board with rubber cement.
- **Step Three:** Saw the frame first; then saw the remaining pieces.
- **Step Four:** Remove all the burs from the backs of the pieces with sandpaper.
- **Step Five:** Transfer the numbers to the bottom of each piece; then carefully pull the paper pattern off the wood.
- **Step Six:** Assemble–but don't glue–the pieces inside the frame; then sand the top of the entire project with 220-grit sandpaper.
- **Step Seven:** Remove the pieces from the frame and round the edges of each piece, including the frame, to about a ⅟₃₂ in. to ⅟₁₆ in. radius. Leave the outer edge of the frame square.
- **Step Eight:** Use a tack cloth to remove any saw dust from the pieces; then paint the sides and edges of each piece according to the color plan.
- **Step Nine:** Glue the frame to the backing. Starting with a corner piece, carefully assemble and glue the pieces in the frame. Add any fine details.
- **Step Ten:** When the glue has dried according to the manufacturer's directions, apply a satin varnish to the entire piece.

Segmentation at a Glance

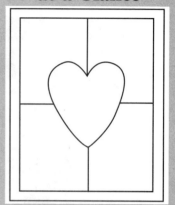

The scene or figure is cut into pieces according to the pattern.

The edges of each piece are rounded, and the pieces are painted.

The rounded, painted pieces are assembled and glued to a ⅛ in. backing.

Black Eyed Susan

Pattern
100%
© Frank Droege

Number	Description	Color
1	frame	bright orange
2	flower center	brown
3–15	flower petals	yellow-orange
16–19	stem and leaves	dark green
20–22	leaves	light green
23–28	background	gold
29–33	background	beige
34–39	background	ivory
40–42	background	yellow

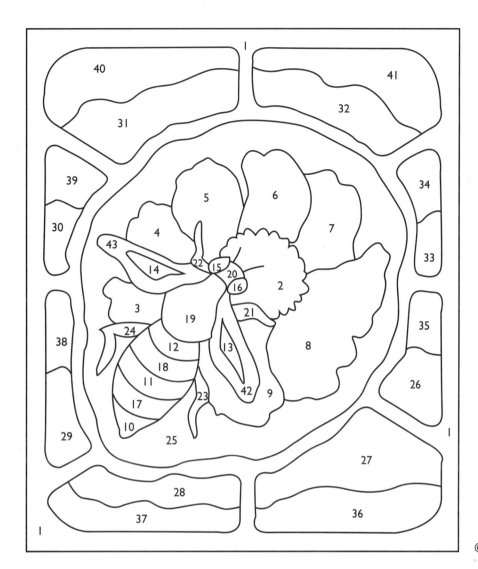

Pattern
100%

© Frank Droege

Number	Description	Color
1	frame	dark brown
2	flower center	gold
3–9	flower petals	salmon
10–16	bee	orange
17–24, 42-43	bee	black
25–33	background	tan
34–41	background	putty

* Paint eyes and woodburn lines for antennae.

Number	Description	Color
1	frame	brown
2	cross	red
3–6	cross	gold
7	background	ivory
8–15	background	pale orange
16–23	background	pale yellow

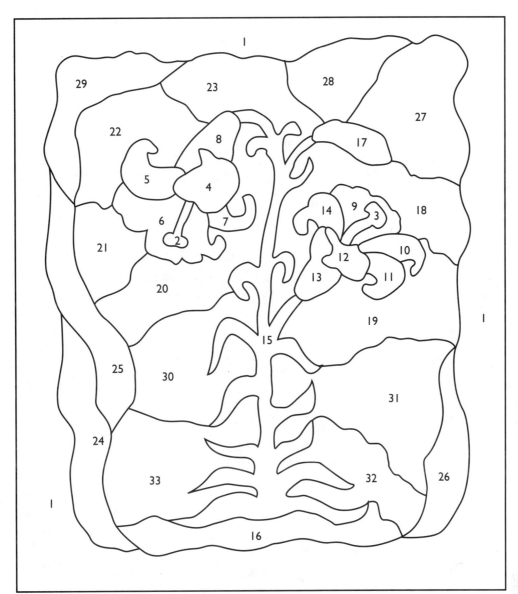

Pattern
100%
© Frank Droege

Number	Description	Color
1	frame	red
2–3	stamens	gold
4–14	flower petals	white
15	stem and leaves	light green
16	grass	dark green
17–23	background	pink
24–28	background	dusty rose
29	background	hot pink
30–33	background	pale pink

Pattern
100%
© Frank Droege

Number	Description	Color
1–2	frame	dark blue
3	boat	brown
4–5	masts	dark brown
6	flag	dark red
7–10	sail, man	white
11–13	sky, waves	dark blue
14–17	sky	blue
18–27	sky, water	lavender
28–31	sky, waves	blue
32	waves	blue-gray
33	sky	dark lavender
34-41	background	black
42–49	background	bright blue

Pattern
100%

© Frank Droege

Number	Description	Color
1	frame	medium blue
2–5	background	dark blue
6–11	background	blue
12–15	background	light blue
16–17	leaves	dark green
18–23	leaves and stem	medium green
24–26	vine	light green
27–32	flower petals	white

Number	Description	Color
33	stamen	yellow
34	flower center	midnight blue
35	stem	light green
36	flower bud	pink
37–38	sun	yellow

Pattern
100%

© Frank Droege

Number	Description	Color
1	frame	very dark blue
2–4	flower petals	yellow-orange
5	flower petals	yellow
6–7	flower petals	pale yellow
8–10	stamen	orange
11–12	calyx	yellow-green
13	calyx	light green
14–16	stem and leaves	dark green
17–20	background	midnight blue
21–22	background	blue
23–24	background	light blue
25	background	slate blue
26–28	background	dark blue
29–31	stars and moon	white

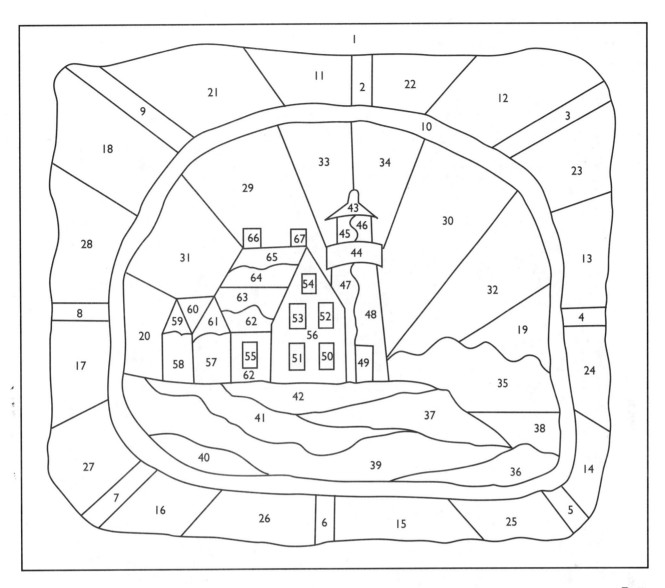

Pattern
100%
© Frank Droege

Number	Description	Color
1–10	frame	very dark blue
11–20	background	pale blue
21–30	background	blue
31–32	background	light blue
33–34	background	dark blue
35	cloud	white
36–37	island	brown
38	ocean	sea blue
39	island	green
40–41	island	pine green
42	island	yellowish brown

Number	Description	Color
43–44	lighthouse	black
45	lighthouse	white
46	lighthouse	pale blue
47	lighthouse	brick red
48	lighthouse	red
49–55	doors and windows	dark brown
56–67	house	shades of brown

Pattern
100%

© Frank Droege

Number	Description	Color
1	outer frame	blue gray
2	inner frame	dark blue
3	lighthouse	white
4	lighthouse	sky blue
5	lighthouse	red-orange
6–8	windows, doors	black
9–10	lighthouse	brick red
11–13	lighthouse	white
14–16	lighthouse	light blue
17	lighthouse	red-orange
18–21	sky	medium blue
22–25	sky	blue

Number	Description	Color
26–27	cloud	white
28–29	sky	sky blue
30–31	sky	pale blue
32–33	ocean	sea blue
34	trees	green
35–36	trees, grass	dark green
37	grass	light green
38	sand	tan
39	path	beige
40–41	ground	dark brown
42	ground	brown

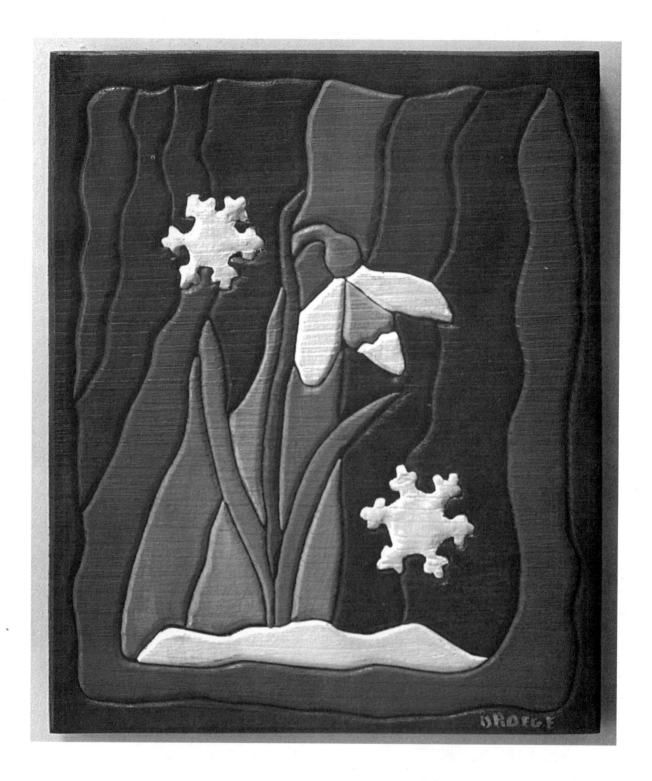

Pattern
100%
© Frank Droege

Number	Description	Color
1–5	frame, background	midnight blue
6–7	background	dark blue
8	background	blue
9	background	light blue
10–11	background	slate blue
12–14	background	pale blue
15	stem	dark green
16–17	leaves	green
18	calyx	yellow-green
19	flower	light yellow-green
20–24	flower petals, snow	white

Flamingo

Pattern
100%

© Frank Droege

Number	Description	Color
1	frame	dark brown
2–3	flamingo	pink
4–5	flamingo	light pink
6–8	flamingo	hot pink
9	eye	light blue
10–11	bill	orange
12–13	water	blue
14–17	water	white
18–19	bushes	green
20–23	shore	tan
24	sky, background	light blue
25–48	background	shades of blue

* Paint pupil of eye.

Dragon Flies

Pattern
100%

© Frank Droege

Number	Description	Color
1	frame	dark brown
2–5	eyes	black
6–11	heads, wings	dark blue
12–15	wings	dark green
16–19	tails	brown
20–22	tails, reeds	green
23	flower center	yellow
24–31	water lily	salmon
32	water	blue
35–50	background	shades of yellow

* Woodburn tails.

Pansy

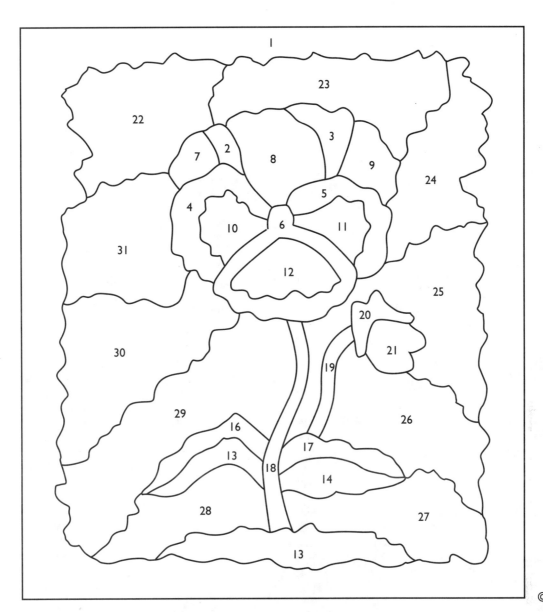

Pattern
100%
© Frank Droege

Number	Description	Color
1	frame	midnight blue
2–6	flower	midnight blue
7–9	flower	blue
10–11	flower	gold
12	flower	yellow
13–15	ground, leaves	dark green
16–17	leaves	green
18–20	stem	light green
21	bird	midnight blue
22–31	background	shades of yellow

Pattern
100%

© Frank Droege

Number	Description	Color
1–2	inside, outside frames	blue
3–4	sail	yellow
5–7	sail	orange
8	sail	red
9–10	people, mast	black
11	boat	white
12–13	boat	brown
14	sky	dark blue
15–16	sky	slate blue
17–18	sky	white
19–28	ocean	shades of blue and green
29–32	background	pink
33–36	background	light blue

* Paint faces of people in boat.

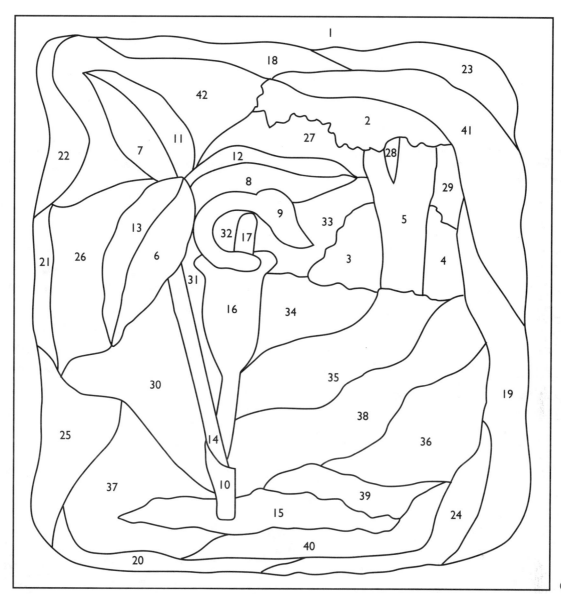

Pattern
100%

© Frank Droege

Number	Description	Color
1	frame	brown
2–4	trees	dark blue green
5	trees	brown
6–10	leaves, stem	dark green
11–15	leaves, stem	green
16	pulpit	light green
17	Jack	white
18–21	background	rust
22–25	background	salmon
26–29	background	light salmon
30–34	background	pink
35–37	background	sand
38–41	background	putty
42	background	hot pink

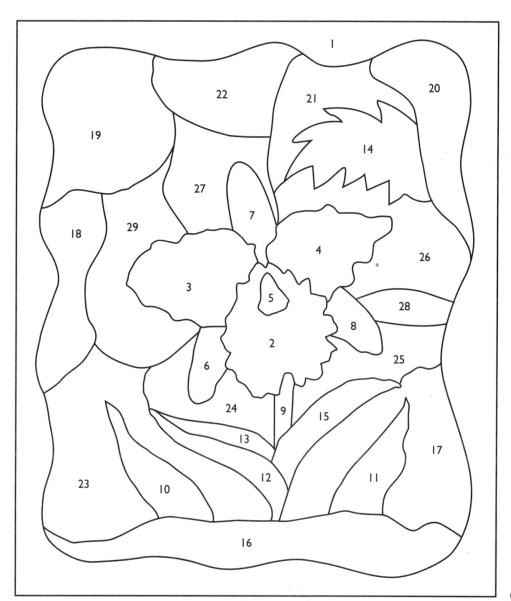

Pattern
100%
© Frank Droege

Number	Description	Color
1	frame	very dark blue
2	flower	purple
3–4	flower	light purple
5	flower	red
6–8	flower	white
9–11	stem, leaves	green
12–14	leaves	dark green
15	leaf	yellow-green
16	ground	very dark green
17–19	background	brown-orange
20	background	orange

Number	Description	Color
21–23	background	yellow-orange
24–27	background	gold
28–29	background	pale yellow

Pattern
100%
© Frank Droege

Number	Description	Color
1	outer frame	dark purple
2	inner frame	gold
3–15	flower	purple
16–20	stem, leaves	dark green
21–26	stem, leaves	green
27–30	background	ivory
31–33	background	yellow
34–37	background	tan
38–39	background	lilac

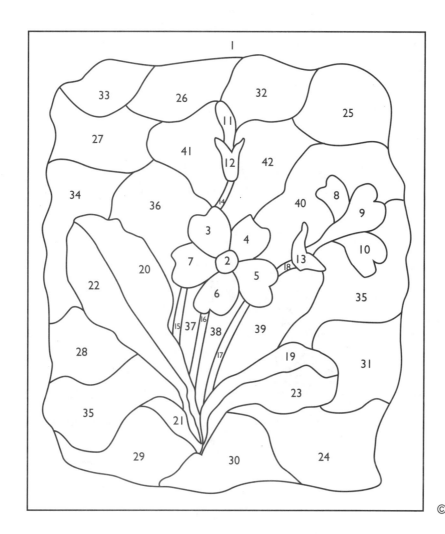

Pattern
100%
© Frank Droege

Number	Description	Color
1	frame	tan
2	flower center	brown
3–7	flower petals	orange
8–10	flower petals	yellow
11	flower petal	dark yellow
12–13	calyx	yellow-green
14–18	stems	light green
19–21	leaf	green
22–23	leaf	dark green
24–29	background	yellow
30–34	background	light blue
35–37	background	blue
38–41	background	pale blue
42	background	blue-gray

**Pattern
100%**

© Frank Droege

Number	Description	Color
1	frame	green
2	flower center	yellow
3–7	flower petals	purple
8–11	flower petals	light purple
12	leaf	very dark green
13	leaf	dark green
14–15	leaf	green
16–17	stem	light green
18–20	background	yellow
21–24	background	yellow-orange
25–26	background	orange

Number	Description	Color
27	background	pink
28–29	background	light pink
30–34	background	tan

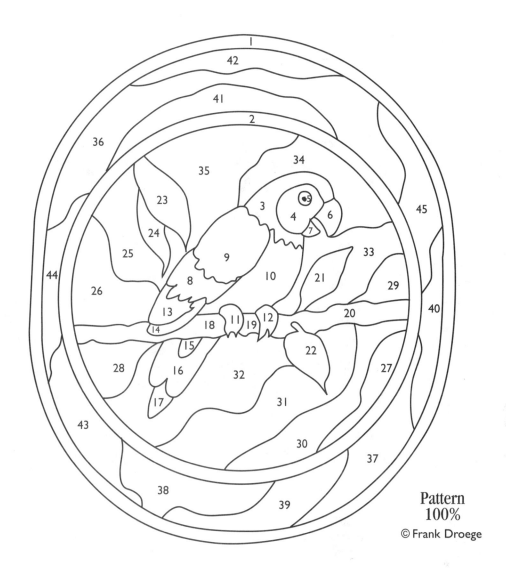

Pattern
100%

© Frank Droege

Number	Description	Color
1	outer frame	dark brown
2	inner frame	very dark brown
3	bird	orange-red
4	bird	white
5–8	bird	yellow
9, 17	bird	red
10	bird	red-brown
11–12	bird	orange
13	bird	blue
14	bird	light blue
15	bird	pale blue
16	bird	dark blue

Number	Description	Color
18–20	branch	very dark green
21–24	leaves	light green
25–29	background	lilac
30	background	medium blue
31	background	pale blue
32	background	blue
33–35	background	shades of light blue
36–38	background	yellow
39–43	background	red
44-45	background	brown

* Paint eye.

Pattern
100%
© Frank Droege

Number	Description	Color
1	frame	dark green
2–4	branch	brown
5–13	grasshopper	light green
14–19	grasshopper	dark green
20–22	grasshopper	green
23–24	grasshopper	blue green
25–26	grasshopper	medium green
27–30, 49-50	background	ivory
31–40	background	pale yellow
41–48	background	yellow
49	eye	black

* Paint eye and woodburn antennae and mouth.

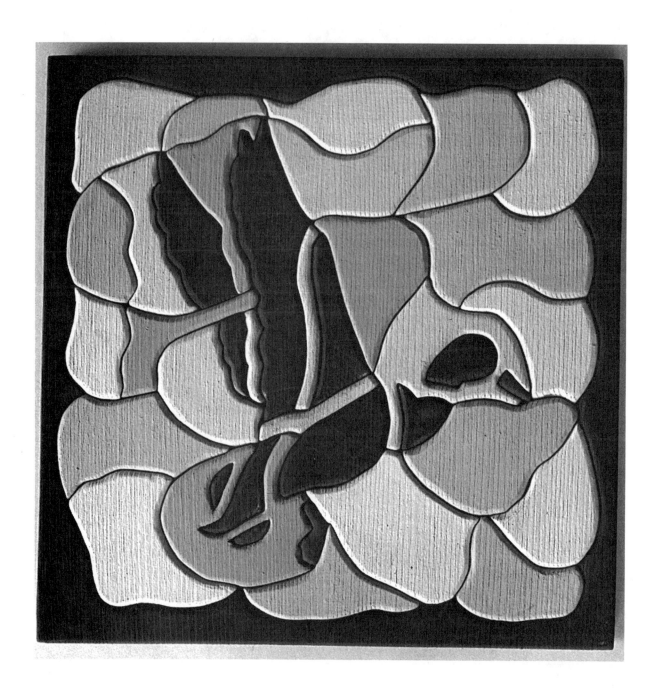

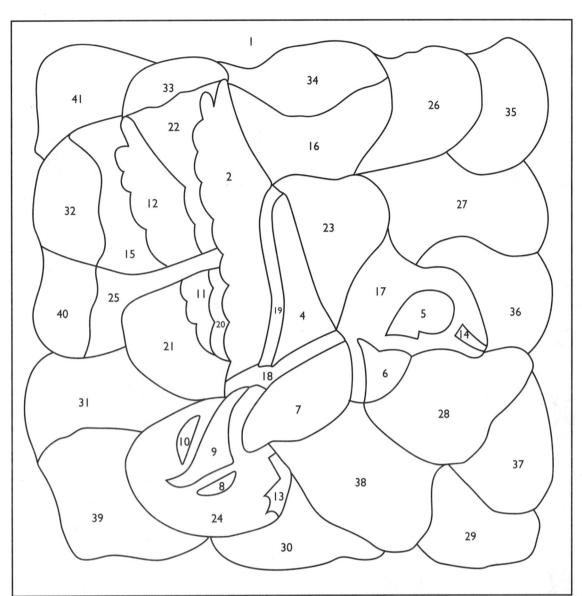

Number	Description	Color
1	frame	brown
2–12	duck	brown
13	foot	red
14	bill	orange
15–21	background	yellow
22–25	background	rose
26–33	background	gray
34–41	background	ivory

Pattern
100%

© Frank Droege

Number	Description	Color
1	frame	blue
2–3	doves	white
4–5	branches	green
6–7	background	bright blue
8–12	background	pale blue
13–17	background	light blue

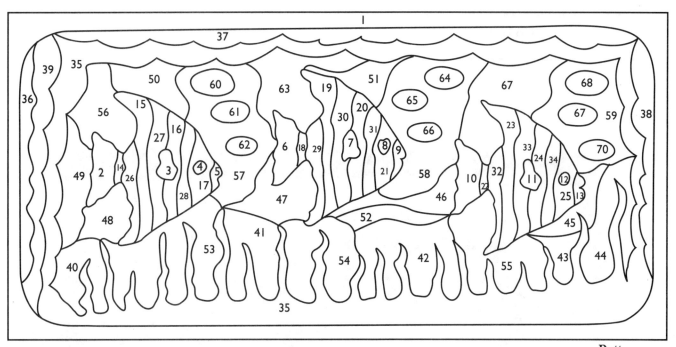

Pattern
100%

© Frank Droege

Number	Description	Color
1	frame	dark green
2–13	fins, tails, eyes, lips	red-orange
14–25	stripes	black
26–34	stripes	yellow
35	seaweed, background	green
36–38	background	light green
39	background	blue-green
40–44	background	dark blue
45–48	background	bright blue
49–52	background	blue
53–55	background	sea blue
56–59	background	light blue
60–70	background	pale blue

* Paint pupils.

Pattern
100%

© Frank Droege

Number	Description	Color
1	outer frame	dark green
2	inner frame	light green
3–8	girl	flesh
9	hat	red
10–11	hair	yellow
12–13	dress	blue
14–15	dress	bright blue
16–17	instrument	dark brown
18	instrument	black
19–20	wings	light yellow-green
21–27	background	pink
28–29	background	light blue

Number	Description	Color
30	background	light blue-green
31–32	background	light yellow-green
33–38	background	green
39–40	background	light green
41–46	background	pale green
47–53	background	yellow
54-57	branches	brown

*Paint circles on wings. Woodburn facial features.

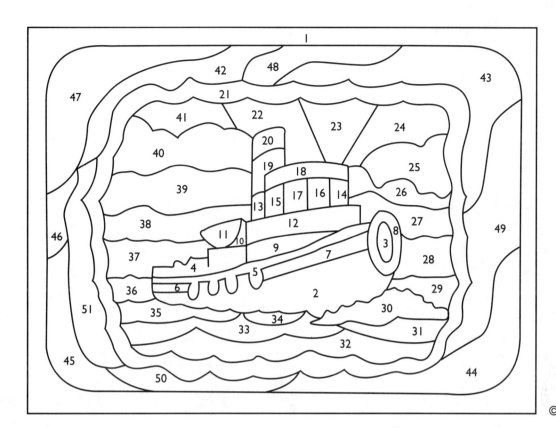

Pattern
100%

© Frank Droege

Number	Description	Color
1	frame	black
2–4	boat	dark brown
5	boat	brown
6–7	boat	dark red
8	boat	light brown
9–10	boat	green
11	boat	white
12	boat	yellow
13–14	boat	blue
15–16	boat	light blue
17	boat	pale blue
18	boat	orange-yellow
19	boat	red
20	boat	black
21–41	ocean	shades of blue, green and white
42–46	background	tan
47–51	background	brown

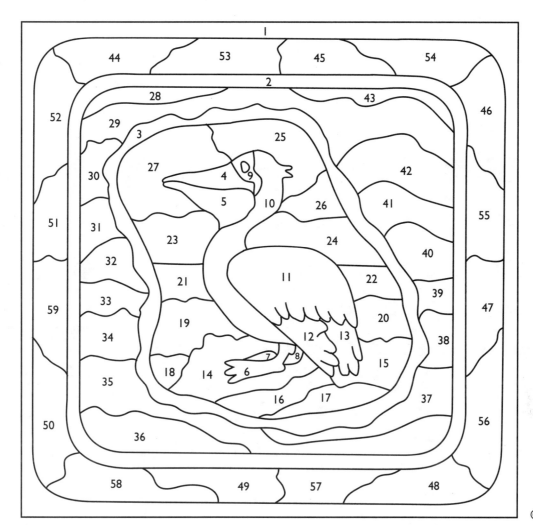

**Pattern
100%**

© Frank Droege

Number	Description	Color
1–2	outer, middle frame	brown
3	inner frame	dark blue
4–8	bill, feet	orange
9	pelican	tan
10	pelican	dark brown
11	pelican	light brown
12–13	pelican	medium brown
14–15	sand	khaki
16	sand	brown
17	sand	dark brown
18	water	dark blue
19–20	water	blue

Number	Description	Color
21–22	water	bright blue
23–25	sky	pale blue
26–27	sky	light blue
28–43	background	shades of brown
44–51	background	light blue
52–59	background	khaki

* Paint eye and pupil.

Pattern
100%

© Frank Droege

Number	Description	Color
1	outer frame	brown
2	inner frame	light brown
3–4	bug	red
5–15	bug	black
16–18	leaf	green
19–21	background	orange
22–24	background	yellow
25–32	background	light green
33–40	background	blue-green

* Paint or cut eyes.

Vase of Flowers

Bouquet of Flowers

Number	Description	Color
1	outer frame	brown
2	background	brown
3	flowers, vase	white
4	inner frame	orange-brown
5–8	background	light brown
9–12	background	yellow

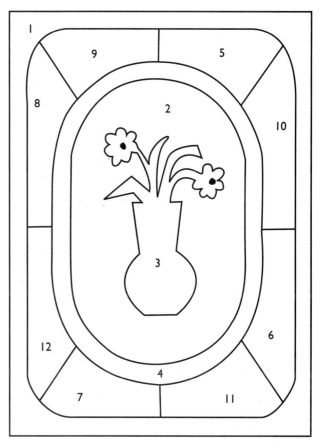

**Pattern
100%**

© Frank Droege

Number	Description	Color
1	frame	dark blue
2–9	flowers	yellow
10	bud	light yellow
11–15	leaves, stems	dark green
16–19	leaves, stems	green
20–21	leaves, stems	light green
22–25	background	light purple

* Paint flower centers.

Option: Paint the backing board light purple and do not use the background pieces.

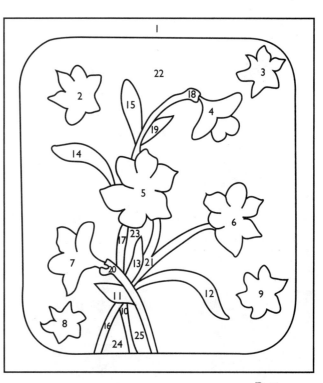

**Pattern
100%**

© Frank Droege